151+
Yo Momma
Jokes

LOL FUNNY JOKES CLUB

Copyright © 2014 LOL FUNNY JOKES CLUB

All rights reserved.

ISBN: 1511768304
ISBN-13: 978-1511768306

CONTENTS

1	**YO MOMMA IS SO FAT...**	1
2	**YO MOMMA IS SO SKINNY...**	Pg #7
3	**YO MOMMA IS SO OLD...**	Pg #9
4	**YO MOMMA IS SO SHORT...**	Pg #11
5	**YO MOMMA IS SO TALL...**	Pg #13
6	**YO MOMMA IS SO POOR...**	Pg #14
7	**YO MOMMA IS SO STUPID...**	Pg #16
8	**YO MOMMA IS SO UGLY...**	Pg #18
9	**YO MOMMA IS SO HAIRY...**	Pg #20
10	**YO MOMMA IS SO BALD...**	Pg #21
11	**YO MOMMA IS SO LAZY...**	Pg #22
12	**OTHER YO MOMMA JOKES...**	Pg #23

1 YO MOMMA IS SO FAT…

Yo momma is so fat… she gives herself group hugs!

Yo momma is so fat… she makes a whale look bulimic!

Yo momma is so fat… she jumped off the Grand Canyon and got stuck.

Yo momma is so fat… when she takes a bath she fills the tub then turns on the water.

Yo momma is so fat… she walked in front of the TV and I missed 3 shows.

Yo momma is so fat… her husband has to stand up in bed each morning to see if it's daylight!

Yo momma is so fat… she fell and made the Grand Canyon!

Yo momma is so fat… every time she walks in high heels, she strikes oil!

Yo momma is so fat… when she jumps up in the air she gets stuck!

Yo momma is so fat… when she bungee jumps she goes straight to hell!

Yo momma is so fat… when she lays on the beach no one else gets sun!

Yo momma is so fat… when she goes to an amusement park, people try to ride her!

Yo momma is so fat… when she plays hopscotch, she goes North America, Europe, Asia.

Yo momma is so fat… NASA has to orbit a satellite around her!

Yo momma is so fat… whenever she goes to the beach the tide comes in!

Yo momma is so fat… she looks like she's smuggling an SUV!

Yo momma is so fat… she's got her own area code!

Yo momma is so fat… when she steps on the scale it says we don't do livestock.

Yo momma is so fat… when she steps on a scale, it read, "one at a time, please".

Yo momma is so fat… the highway patrol made her wear "Caution! Wide Turn!"

Yo momma is so fat… when she bungee jumps, she brings down the bridge too.

Yo momma is so fat... she put on her lipstick with a paint roller.

Yo momma is so fat... she goes to a restaurant, looks at the menu, and says, "okay!"

Yo momma is so fat... when she has wants someone to shake her hand, she has to give directions!

Yo momma is so fat... she lays on the beach and people run around yelling Free Willy!

Yo momma is so fat... she was floating in the ocean and Spain claimed her for the new world!

Yo momma is so fat... she went to the movies and sat next to everyone.

Yo momma is so fat... she eats Wheat Thicks.

Yo momma is so fat... people jog around her for exercise.

Yo momma is so fat... her nickname is Lardo.

Yo momma is so fat... when her beeper goes off, people think she is backing up.

Yo momma is so fat... the back of her neck is like a pack of hot dogs!

Yo momma is so fat... when she gets on the elevator it says, "Next stop, Hell"!

Yo momma is so fat... she sat on a tractor and made a pick-up truck.

Yo momma is so fat… when she dives into the ocean, there is a tsunami-warning!

Yo momma is so fat… that when she wanted a waterbed, they had to put a cover over the Atlantic Ocean.

Yo momma is so fat… that she needs a bookmark to keep track of all her chin rolls!

Yo momma is so fat… she sat on a rainbow and made skittles.

Yo momma is so fat… she had to be baptized at sea world.

Yo momma is so fat… it took me a bus and two trains just to get on her good side.

Yo momma is so fat… she uses an air balloon for a parachute.

Yo momma is so fat… she was going to Wal-Mart, tripped over Kmart, and landed right on Target!!!

Yo momma is so fat… her measurements are 26-34-28, and her other arm is just as big!

Yo momma is so fat… she broke a branch in her family tree!

Yo momma is so fat… when she wore a blue and green sweater, everyone thought she was Planet Earth.

Yo momma is so fat… she makes Godzilla look like an action figure.

Yo momma is so fat… when she took her shirt off at the strip club, everyone thought she was Jabber the Hut from Star Wars.

Yo momma is so fat… when she was in school she sat next to everybody!

Yo momma is so fat… when she went bungee jumping in a yellow dress, everyone was screaming the suns falling!

Yo momma is so fat… she had her ears pierced by harpoon.

Yo momma is so fat… she needs a watch on both arms because she covers two time zones.

Yo momma is so fat… when she turns around they throw her a welcome back party.

Yo momma is so fat… she sank the Titanic!

Yo momma is so fat… when she sits on the beach, whales swim up to her and sing we are family…!

Yo momma is so fat… when she wears a red dress all the kids scream look it's the Kool-Aid man.

Yo momma is so fat… the last time she saw 90210 was on the scale!

Yo momma is so fat… when you go around her you get lost!

Yo momma is so fat… she has seat belts on the chairs to keep her fat from rolling off!

Yo momma is so fat… they had to install speed bumps

at all you can eat buffets.

Yo momma is so fat… when a bus hit her she said, "Who threw the pebble?"

Yo momma is so fat… when she puts on her yellow rain coat and walks down the street people shout out "taxi"!

Yo momma is so fat… she uses the interstate as a slip and slide.

Yo momma is so fat… you could use her bellybutton as a wishing well.

Yo momma is so fat… the government forced her to wear taillights and blinkers so no one else would get hurt.

Yo momma is so fat… she supplies 99% of the world's gas.

Yo momma is so fat… when she goes to Taco Bell, they run for the border!

Yo momma is so fat… she rolled out of bed and everybody thought there was an earthquake.

Yo momma is so fat… when God said, "Let there be light," he had to ask her to move out of the way.

Yo momma is so fat… she has more chins than a Chinese phone book.

Yo momma is so fat… she jumped in the air and got stuck.

Yo momma is so fat… she's got to wake up in sections.

2 YO MOMMA IS SO SKINNY…

Yo momma is so skinny… she can hang glide with a Dorito!

Yo momma is so skinny… she swallowed a meatball and thought she was pregnant.

Yo momma is so skinny… she turned sideways and disappeared.

Yo momma is so skinny… she hula hoops with a cheerio.

Yo momma is so skinny… she has to run around in the shower just to get wet.

Yo momma is so skinny… she don't get wet when it rains.

Yo momma is so skinny… her nipples touch.

Yo momma is so skinny… she has to wear a belt with her spandex pants.

Yo momma is so skinny… she can see through peepholes with both eyes.

Yo momma is so skinny… she can dive through a chain-linked fence.

Yo momma is so skinny… she uses cotton balls for pillows.

3 YO MOMMA IS SO OLD…

Yo momma is so old… she knew the Great Wall of China when it was only good!

Yo momma is so old… that her bus pass is in hieroglyphics!

Yo momma is so old… she was wearing a Jesus starter jacket!

Yo momma is so old… her birth certificate is in Roman numerals.

Yo momma is so old… she ran track with dinosaurs.

Yo momma is so old… she knew Burger King while he was still a prince.

Yo momma is so old… her birth certificate says expired on it.

Yo momma is so old… she has a picture of Moses in her yearbook.

Yo momma is so old… that when she was in school there was no history class.

Yo momma is so old… her social security number is 1!

Yo momma is so old… I told her to act her own age, and she died.

4 YO MOMMA IS SO SHORT…

Yo momma is so short… she does backflips under the bed.

Yo momma is so short … she can play handball on the curb.

Yo momma is so short… she can use a sock for a sleeping bag.

Yo momma is so short… she can tie her shoes while standing up.

Yo momma is so short… she can sit on a dime and swing her legs.

Yo momma is so short … she has to use a ladder to pick up a dime.

Yo momma is so short … she poses for trophies!

Yo momma is so short… she has a job as a teller at a piggy bank.

Yo momma is so short… she has to use rice to roll her hair up.

Yo momma is so short… she uses a toothpick as pool stick.

Yo momma is so short… she can surf on a popsicle stick.

5 YO MOMMA IS SO TALL...

Yo momma is so tall... she tripped in Denver and hit her head in New York.

Yo momma is so tall... she tripped over a rock and hit her head on the moon.

Yo momma is so tall... Shaq looks up to her.

Yo momma is so tall... she can see her home from anywhere.

Yo momma is so tall... she 69'd bigfoot.

Yo momma is so tall... she did a cartwheel and kicked the gates of Heaven.

Yo momma is so tall... she has to take a bath in the ocean.

Yo momma is so tall... she high-fived God.

6 YO MOMMA IS SO POOR…

Yo momma is so poor… your family ate cereal with a fork to save milk.

Yo momma is so poor… the roaches pay the light bill!

Yo momma is so poor… I walked in her house and stepped on a cigarette, and your mom said, "Who turned off the lights?"

Yo momma is so poor… when her friend came over to use the bathroom she said, "Ok, choose a corner."

Yo momma is so poor… I stepped in her house and I was in the backyard.

Yo momma is so poor… she waves around a popsicle stick and calls it air conditioning.

Yo momma is so poor… she was in K-Mart with a box of Hefty bags. I said, what ya doing'? She said, "Buying luggage."

Yo momma is so poor... when I ring the doorbell she says, DING!

Yo momma is so poor... she can't afford to pay attention!

Yo momma is so poor... when I saw her kicking a can down the street, I asked her what she was doing, she said, "Moving."

7 YO MOMMA IS SO STUPID…

Yo momma is so stupid… she can't pass a blood test.

Yo momma is so stupid… she ordered a cheeseburger without the cheese.

Yo momma is so stupid… that she burned down the house with a CD burner.

Yo momma is so stupid… she got locked in a grocery store and starved.

Yo momma is so stupid… when they said that it is chilly outside, she went outside with a bowl and a spoon.

Yo momma is so stupid… she got lost in a telephone booth.

Yo momma is so stupid… she put lipstick on her forehead to make up her mind.

Yo momma is so stupid… she got locked in Furniture World and slept on the floor.

Yo momma is so stupid… she sits on the floor and watches the couch.

Yo momma is so stupid… she stole free bread.

Yo momma is so stupid… she sold her car for gas money.

Yo momma is so stupid… she worked at a M&M factory and threw out all the W's.

Yo momma is so stupid… she tried to commit suicide by jumping out the basement window.

Yo momma is so stupid… she stopped at a stop sign and waited for it to turn green.

Yo momma is so stupid… when she asked me what kind of jeans am I wearing I said, "Guess", and she said, "Levis".

Yo momma is so stupid… it took her two hours to watch 60 seconds.

8 YO MOMMA IS SO UGLY…

Yo momma is so ugly… that your father takes her to work with him so that he doesn't have to kiss her goodbye.

Yo momma is so ugly… The NHL banned her for life.

Yo momma is so ugly… she turned Medusa to stone!

Yo momma is so ugly… for Halloween she trick-or-treats on the phone!

Yo momma is so ugly… even Rice Krispies won't talk to her!

Yo momma is so ugly… she tried to take a bath and the water jumped out!

Yo momma is so ugly… when they took her to the beautician it took 12 hours for a quote!

Yo momma is so ugly… she made an onion cry.

Yo momma is so ugly… when she walks down the

street in September, people say "Wow, is it Halloween already?"

Yo momma is so ugly… her mom had to tie a steak around her neck to get the dogs to play with her.

Yo momma is so ugly… when she walks into a bank, they turn off the surveillance cameras.

Yo momma is so ugly… she gets 364 extra days to dress up for Halloween.

Yo momma is so ugly… instead of putting the bungee cord around her ankle, they put it around her neck.

Yo momma is so ugly… they didn't give her a costume when she tried out for Star Wars.

Yo momma is so ugly… just after she was born, her mother said, "What a treasure!" And her father said, "Yes, let's go bury it!"

Yo momma is so ugly… when she joined an ugly contest, they said, "Sorry, no professionals."

Yo momma is so ugly… that she scares blind people!

Yo momma is so ugly… she got beat up by her imaginary friends!

Yo momma is so ugly… the government moved Halloween to her birthday.

9 YO MOMMA IS SO HAIRY…

Yo momma is so hairy… you almost died of rug burn at birth!

Yo momma is so hairy… she wears a Nike tag on her weave so now everybody calls her Hair Jordan.

Yo momma is so hairy… that Bigfoot tried to take her picture!

Yo momma is so hairy… Harry Potter got jealous.

Yo momma is so hairy… her tits look like coconuts.

Yo momma is so hairy… she shaves with a weed-eater.

Yo momma is so hairy… the zoo offered to buy her kids.

Yo momma is so hairy… she has cornrows on her back, legs, and feet!

10 YO MOMMA IS SO BALD...

Yo momma is so bald… that she took a shower and got brainwashed.

Yo momma is so bald… you can see what's on her mind.

Yo momma is so bald… even a wig wouldn't help!

Yo momma is so bald… Mr. Clean was jealous.

Yo momma is so bald… she braids her beard.

Yo momma is so bald… everyone thought the sun was rising when she got up.

11 YO MOMMA IS SO LAZY…

Yo momma is so lazy… that she came in last place in a recent snail marathon.

Yo momma is so lazy… she's got a remote control just to operate her remote!

Yo momma is so lazy… she thinks a two-income family is where the man has two jobs.

Yo momma is so lazy… she arrived late at her own funeral.

Yo momma is so lazy… she starved instead of getting up to get some food.

12 OTHER YO MOMMA JOKES...

Yo momma's teeth are so yellow... that when she smiles everyone sings, "I got sunshine on a cloudy day."

Yo momma's teeth are so yellow... I can't believe it's not butter.

Yo momma's teeth are so yellow... that when she smiles traffic slows down.

Yo momma ain't got no ears yelling... Let me hear both sides of the story!

Yo momma's head is so big... she has to step into her shirts.

Yo momma is like the sun... you look at her to long you will go blind!

Yo momma's house is so poor... I went to knock on her door and a roach tripped me and a rat took my wallet!

Yo momma's house is so small... you have to go

outside to change your mind.

Yo momma's feet are so scaly… you can see Crocodile Dundy in her footbath.

Yo momma is in a wheelchair and says… "You ain't gonna push me around no more!"

Yo momma is so small… that she got her ear pierced and died.

Yo momma's head is so small… she uses a tea bag as a pillow.

Yo momma's nose is so big… that her neck broke from the weight!

Yo momma's nose is so big… she makes Pinocchio look like a cat!

Yo momma's house is so small… that when she orders a large pizza she had to go outside to eat it.

Yo momma's glasses are so thick… she can see into the future.

Yo momma's glasses are so thick… that when she looks on a map she can see people waving.

Yo momma's head is so big… it shows up on radar.

Yo momma is so nasty… cows with mad cow disease run from her.

Yo momma's feet are so big… her shoes have to have license plates!

Yo momma's mouth is so big… she speaks in surround sound.

Yo momma has so many chins… it looks like she's wearing a fat necklace!

Yo momma is so clumsy… she got tangled up in a cordless phone.

Yo momma is so grouchy… the McDonald's she works at doesn't even serve happy meals.

Yo momma is cross-eyed and watches TV in stereo.

Yo momma is missing a finger and can't count past nine.

Yo momma's middle name is Rambo.

LOL FUNNY JOKES CLUB

The LOL Funny Jokes Club is dedicated to comedy. We'll tickle your funny bone with our side-splitting jokes and humor. Whether it's funny one-liners hilarious jokes, or laugh-out-loud rib tickling knee slappers, the LOL Funny Jokes Club does it all!

To find more funny and hilarious joke books just search for LOL FUNNY JOKES CLUB on Amazon.com.

Made in the USA
Columbia, SC
19 November 2018